# FRAGILE

## THE BROKEN HEARTS

## SADHU HARSHA VARDHAN

A TRUE LOVE WILL NEVER FADE AWAY

# Contents

# Foreword

GET READY TO FEEL THE GREATEST LOVE STORY EVER

• vii •

# Preface

A misunderstanding. That is all it took to break Shehryaar and Leila apart, who were once so in love and now they hated each other's guts. When the truth comes out, all Shehryaar needed was a second chance. A chance which Leila was not sure if she can give. Join in to know what caused them to break apart and how they fight against the odds for their happy ending.

# Acknowledgements

DEDICATED TO THE TRUE LOVES OUT THERE WITH LOVE FOR CHITTI THALLI

# Prologue

" A single misunderstanding is so poisonous, that it makes us forget the hundred lovable moments spent within a minute."

# ONE
# CHAPTER 01

" A single misunderstanding is so poisonous, that it makes us forget the hundred lovable moments spent within a minute."

***

The bright rays of sunlights peeped into her room disturbing her beautiful sleep. Leila Qureshi wasn't a fan of waking up early but she does it anyway, she cannot go and change the college timings from 12:00 to 13:00 now, can she? Although she wishes that she could. Soon enough her alarm too started to ring which she dismissed with a sigh and got up to do her morning routine.

After getting dressed in an off-white Kurti, matched with a blue coloured dupatta; she descends downstairs with a frown on her face. There was this test in her college today which she didn't bother to prepare and now she regrets not studying earlier. But the frown disappears as soon as the smell of aloo paratha hits her nostrils.

"Aslamualaikum, ammi!" Leila greeted her mother with a happy smile and grabs one paratha from the hot box and savours it without any second thoughts.

"Walaikumaslam, Leila. Eat slowly." Humera Qureshi smiled at her dear daughter as she continued to prepare the parathas. Leila smiled back as she continued to stuff the paratha into her mouth. She loves her ammi's handmade parathas and according to her, they are the world's best parathas.

"Tayi ammi, bee jaan is asking you to prepare the breakfast quickly. Shehryaar is going somewhere early today." a new voice informed Humera, who just entered the kitchen with a bright smile on her face. Leila's frown reappeared as soon as she heard the annoying voice of her cousin, she didn't fail to notice the stress Armeena made while taking Sheryaar's name, which she assumed was for getting a reaction out of her. She didn't care anyway, all that matters to her at that moment was her favourite aloo paratha; which she's busy munching happily.

"It's done now, help me, girls," Humera orders them both with an inward sigh and the other girl excitedly obliged as she helped Humera carry the breakfast to the dining table. Leila didn't bother to do anything as she continued to eat without the care in the world.

If there is anything which Leila hated then that would be Shehryaar Qureshi, her Taya Jaan's son who she hated with every fibre of her body and then comes Armeena Quershi, her Chacha Jaan's daughter, who she hated as equally or more.

"Leila, I asked you to help me." Humera who came back from the dining room glared at her daughter in disappointment who washed her hands in a hurry.

"Ammi, even after knowing that I hate that guy why are you bothering to make me do stuff for him? After everything he did to me, you should hate him." Exclaimed Leila in disbelief as she frowned at her mother.

"It's been a year now, Leila, why don't you kids move on? The elders are getting affected because of your immature behaviours." Leila so wanted to roll her eyes but she stopped herself.

"I'm getting late, ammi. Don't stress yourself, anyways I don't think that he'd eat the food touched by me. I know him" Leila said with a slight hurt in her voice but masked her emotions quickly as she kissed her mother's cheeks and murmured," Allah Hafiz. I'm getting late now."

"Go safely, Azim Bhai will get your lunch." Humera sighed as she watched her daughter hum in response and leave the kitchen. Azim was their servant who brings lunch for her every day. Leila always gets hot and tasty meals as lunch every single day. She was a little spoiled like that.

The mother-daughter duo was so oblivious to the fact that there was someone else as well who had listened to their conversation; unintentionally. Shehryaar stared at the disappearing image of Leila with a frown on his face. What did that girl think of him anyway? Sure he hates her. But he wouldn't go that far as not eating the food just because she has touched it. It just proved that she didn't know him at all, he wondered how were they once so in love and now how everything has changed. He'd blame Leila for all of the happenings. He'd blame only her.

Leila sighed in relief as she exited her college with a smile on her face. Her mood was whole better compared to the morning. The professor has taken a leave today, meaning; no tests and she has escaped for now. Mentally preparing herself for studying tonight she waited for her driver to arrive.

"Myra. Send me your dress' pictures, I want to see them." she told her best friend excitedly who beamed at her in response.

"Sure. I'm so excited about the wedding." Myra exclaimed in excitement.

"Ohmigod same. I haven't shopped yet, I'm surprised that ammi and abbu are letting me come, all thanks to you. If not they'd never agree to send me that far anyways." Leila said happily but was confused as she saw her friend staring somewhere else.

"Look there, Ibrahim is coming here again with his roses." Myra nudged her friend, whose face paled as soon as she heard that.

"Why don't he quits it? I told him 'n' number of times that I'm not interested." Leila frowned but stopped midway as Ibrahim one of their classmates came close to her with his gorgeous smile plastered on his lips.

"Red roses for the most beautiful girl I've ever seen in my life." Ibrahim forwarded the roses to her, she glared at him in return.

"Quit bothering me, Ibrahim." that guy never took no for an answer and he was behind Leila for the past few months pestering her to go on a date. He was stubborn like that.

"At least take this rose. I've wasted my money on it." Ibrahim decided to guilt trick her but what came next surprised everyone else. Leila gasped in shock with her widened eyes as she watched Shehryaar hit Ibrahim with a force.

"Shehryaar... Get off him." Leila tried to drag her stupid cousin, who was making an unnecessary scene in front of the whole college and it's going to be the gossip of the month. She was handling it just fine.

Just as she expected the whole student group stopped what they were doing and stared at the scenario with gasps and murmurs. Leila groaned in annoyance. Why was Sherhryaar hell-bent on taking away her peace? The home was not enough and now college too. Ugh, she hated him. Hated him so damn much.

Shehryaar didn't bother to stop as he hit Ibrahim mercilessly, the images of this guy giving his Leila roses made him burn with rage and the possessive side of him overtook his emotions and he couldn't just get himself to stop.

"ENOUGH NOW." Leila's angry and loud voice at last stopped him as he stared at the poor guy with rage," you! Stay away from her." he warned that guy who nodded and ran away from there.

"Drama is over. Go away you all."She yelled at no one in particular which made the group formed around them disappear.

"Uh, Leila. My driver is here. See you tomorrow. Allah Hafiz." Myra whispered to her friend as she nodded her head and now it was just him and her.

She glared at him with annoyance, her big doe like eyes seethed with anger. He didn't seem to affect though.

"What is wrong with you?" She whisper yelled at him, conscious at her voice as they still had audience watching them with curiosity.

"Stop being so ungrateful, I was just helping you." Shehryaar rolled his eyes in disbelief, she gave him a pointed stare and decided to just walk away from there. It was pointless talking with him anyway.

"Where are you going now?" he followed her from behind and caught hold of her wrists as he made her stop, she flinched at his touch making him take off his hands almost immediately. He wouldn't lie; it hurt him so much.

"Stop touching me," Leila told whilst gritting her teeth. This made him furious if anything. He can't believe that she was the same Leila whom he fell in love with.

"Why are you here anyway? Where's my driver?" she looked around to find her car, but it was nowhere to be found. She could only see his car and no, she's not getting into that.

"The driver's wife is sick and bee Jaan asked me to pick you for today as it's beside my workplace. I wasn't dying to come here as well." Shehryaar replied with annoyance.

"Of course." she should have known already, the driver did mention about his wife in the morning.

"What was that scene about? I was managing it just fine." she whisper yelled at him as he stared back her with disbelief. Was she serious?

"I was helping you, damn it. You should be thankful to me."

"I don't want your help, Shehryaar Qureshi. Get that straight to your mind."

"Who are you to me anyway? Why do you even care? You're not my fiance. Not anymore at least." she threw those words directly at his face making him freeze for a second.

Yes. She's not his fiancée. She's not his Leila anymore. He has forgotten about that for a moment there, trust her to keep reminding him again and again.

"You're my cousin and don't think that I was doing that for you. I did that for saving my family's reputation." Shehryaar muttered making her give him a blank stare.2

"Yeah sure.I am not coming home with you. Go away from here. I'll take a cab." Leila stated as if its the most obvious thing and took out her phone to book an Uber. His eyes snapped at her words and he snatched her phone from her hands, she looked at him with anger.

"Excuse me?"

"Get in the car. Leila." she glared at him whilst trying to get back her phone, which he held high.

"Get. In.The.Damn.Car." he told each word with pressure and she gave up with a frown.

The ride back home happened in silence as none of them spoke anything else. They'd just glance at each other without the other person noticing.

Leila found it suffocating to be with him in the same place for more than three minutes. They haven't been this close for a long time now and it was starting to bother her. It's almost a year now and she didn't want to be near him anymore. Funny how things changed.

Sometimes two people need to fall apart to realise how much they need to fall back together.

# TWO
## CHAPTER 02

True love has a habit of coming back.

***

Shehryaar couldn't wait to get out of the car already, seeing their villa which was just a minute away made him sigh in relief. Staying with her so close like that after so long made him feel awkward, to say the least, he was sure that the feelings must be mutual too. That made him drive faster if anything. Just as he halted the car before the gate, Leila jumped out at the first chance she got. Shutting the car door with a thud, she entered their entrance while he honked loudly to get the Watchman out to open the door for him.

She could have done that at least, in fact, she used to do it for him after their every long drive and now she doesn't even care to see if he came in or not. What went wrong anyway? Why in the world was she showing him attitude when it was her because of whom they weren't together today.

If only she had been loyal and not cheated on him just two nights before their marriage, things would have been so different now. They would be together living their fantasy but she had to ruin it like that.18

Shehryaar hated her ever since. Or so he told himself. Breathing in and breathing out, he tried to control his rage. After parking his car in the garage, he got down from his car and something bright caught his eyes. He picked it up curiously and realized that it was her phone, which he had snatched near her college.

The memories of that guy giving her a rose came back in a jiffy and he counted numbers this time. He'd do it every time he loses his cool and when he is around Leila Qureshi he had to do these little tricks time and again. She tested his patience like no one else could.

Staring at the phone for longer than a minute made him realize that Leila still hasn't changed her phone case. He had gifted it to her when she turned eighteen and it shocked him to see her still using the same one. She's twenty-two now. Why did she keep that with her? The question rang into his ears again and again as he walked into the villa, trying to distract his stupid brain.

As if on cue, her phone started to ring making him startled. He gazed at the caller ID with a frown and stood nearby the steps sceptically deciding whether or not to go to the west wing of their villa. It belonged to his Chacha Jaan and his family, he hadn't stepped on that side of that house for over a year now.

"Shehryaar... You want something?" Faik Qureshi asked his nephew with a confused face. It shocked him to see that Shehryaar was standing beside his side of the house; willingly. If he hadn't interrupted maybe he might have stepped in too. Faik wondered how did the miracle ever happen.

"Chacha Jaan, Leila has left her phone in the car." Shoving the phone into Faik's hands he marched away from there. As if him standing beside his side of the house was not shocking enough, Leila and Shehryaar coming home together was another big shocker. Curious to find out what happened, Faik Qureshi walked to his daughter's bedroom and knocked at her door.

"Abbu..." Leila was surprised to find her father standing out of her door, she welcomed in with a warm smile. He patted her head affectionately as both the father and daughter sat on the sofa.

"Your phone." Faik gave it to her with a chuckle as he stared at his daughter's questioning gaze. She wanted to ask him why he here but couldn't get herself to ask that. He knew his daughter too well.

"Don't look at me like that. I'm as confused as you." Leila frowned as she took her phone. She still wondered why would Shehryaar willingly come to pick her up from the college.

After a terrible car accident when she was seven, Eirenae's life got turned upside down. Her father changed everything, becoming rotten and abusive to the point it cause...

"Something must have happened then." Faik mused to which she sighed and began to narrate the happenings in the college.

"He still cares for you, Leila," Faik muttered with an amused smile on his face. Yes, it was shocking but from what his daughter said it was crystal clear that Shehryaar cared.

"He confuses me so much, abbu." Leila huffed with annoyance and saw her father laugh at her state.

"And you're making fun of me now."

"No... I'm happy that he's warming up to you. Maybe then you could explain what happened that night and clear things with him." Faik said with a sad smile and the colour on her face paled almost instantly.

"No way, abbu. No way. I'm not doing anything much." Leila muttered sternly and Faik knew how stubborn his daughter can get, so he let it go for now. But this topic would be discussed again and by the next, he'd make sure to clear his daughter's name from the false allegations which they've set up on her. He still doesn't know who it was (his daughter has requested him to leave the matter as it is), he trusted Leila and knew that she can never be disloyal to anyone, let alone cheat. It was so out of the question.

"But you still love him. I can see it in your eyes." Faik felt sorry for his daughter, to be so in love with someone and not being trusted by him was such a hard thing to cope up with but his daughter was doing just fine. She's a brave woman and he was so proud to have her as his daughter. Blood-related or not was not important.

"But he doesn't trust me, abbu. A relationship without trust never works out." Leila sighed sadly. It still hurt her to know that he trusted all the setups against her but not her. To hell with his love, Leila treasures her self respect very much and when he humiliated her for cheating on him, she didn't bother to give him an earful. She just left. It was a waste, she thought.

Looking back at the memories has made her bitter as a drop of tear rolled down her cheeks. She wiped them off almost instantly but it did go by her father's notice.

"Let's go downstairs. It's chai time now." Faik said affectionately, she nodded her head. Maybe that could help her distract her mind. A cup of tea can make miracles happen, at least for her.3

***

Leila was aware of his intense gaze upon her, she could feel it. But she didn't dare look up at him. Not when she was feeling so low all of a sudden. If she by chance gazed at him, then she'd break down or something. Everyone thinks that she was very strong but only she knew how very wrong it was.

"Ammi... I was thinking with Leila's last semester approaching nearby...." Trailing off sceptically Faik continued," I wanted to get her married soon."

This gained everyone's attention. The whole Qureshi family froze at his words. Shehryaar was more shocked than everyone else.

Armeena and her parents, Saad and Mahira waited for some sort of drama.

Sara Qureshi stared at her son, Shehryaar; who didn't bother to mask his shock and surprise. Her husband, Hamad passed his son a sideways glance and then looked at his younger brother to continue.

"If your daughter is okay. Then sure, we will get her married." Agha Jaan had an unusual smile on his face today. Shehryaar snapped his head at that. Seriously? He thought.

"I'm okay with anything." Leila shrugged nonchalantly as she sipped her tea. Bee Jaan stared at her grandchildren with a sad smile. If this was on their fates, who can change it anyway?

"We know a good guy, their family has sent a proposal last week and they want to visit us tomorrow," Humera said excitedly as she smiled widely at her daughter. Leila half smiled and continued to drink her tea.

"Very well then. What are you waiting for? Start the preparations." Agha Jaan ordered sternly as he got up from his seat. Everyone nodded their head except for Shehryaar and Leila.

Shehryaar stared at Laila once again, furiously this time. She was sitting in there so unaffectedly that it was starting to bother him very much.

Was it so easy for her to move on like that? while he's dying from within every single day. He needed answers and he'd get them today, at any costs.

He didn't get his answers back then but today he will.

Everybody has that one person, who they'll never lose feelings for.

# THREE
## CHAPTER 03

When it's real, you can't just walk away.
***


Leila Qureshi was anxious. She couldn't sit straight but sat down anyway. The curious and intense glances from her probably to-be in-laws made her nervous and so freaking anxious. She was more and more self-conscious with each passing second. After being rejected by the love of her life just two days before their marriage has made her somewhat insecure and she couldn't even help about it.

"We love your daughter, she's so pretty Masha Allah." Zoya Khaled exclaimed in glee as she sipped the ginger tea. Humera and Faik passed each happy smiles while Leila sat there numbly whilst thinking; I'm really getting married to someone else then.

"We should not waste any time and conduct the nikkah as soon as possible." To everyone's surprise, it was Agha Jaan who said those words. The whole Qureshi family were shocked yet again. Basheer Qureshi never liked Leila before, he made that clear to everyone else and his sudden interest in getting Leila married made them a little suspicious but they couldn't ponder more on it as Usman Khaled started to talk again.

"We were thinking of doing the same, Junaid has to go back to Seattle next month and we want to get him married soon and pass on the responsibility of taking care of him to my daughter in law." Both families shared a good laugh at Usman Khaled's words except for two people.

Any other girl would have probably blushed but Leila felt nothing. She felt nothing.

Shehryaar felt himself going insane with each passing second. He couldn't fathom the thought that all of this was actually happening in real. His Leila; the love of his life was going to get married but not with him. That was driving him nuts and whatnot but what he couldn't understand was; his feelings. Did he really hate her that much to let her go away? His mind was screaming a big yes but don't even ask about what his heart wanted.

"We will discuss the dates in the phone call then. With our elder's consent and all." Zoya chirped happily as she eyed her son, who was smiling at his mother and father and subtly eyed his future wife, God! She was so beautiful.

"Sure, but let it be as soon as possible." Agha Jaan added once again shocking everyone. They wondered what's wrong with him?

But Leila knew exactly why he was doing this. She couldn't be more disgusted anyways. From the corner of her eyes, she also saw Armeena passing a smug smile on her way. She rolled her eyes at that witch.3

If the saying; 'every dog has its day' was true then Leila wondered when her day would come. She waited for the krama to hit them hard, so badly.

Soon enough the guests left, Leila heaved a sigh of relief, she wouldn't have lasted anymore second pretending to be happy when she is not. Her mother and father have gone with the Khaled's to send them off and everyone else too retreated to their bedroom. Before she could walk upstairs, a strong pair of hands pulled her wrists and she was dragged into the storeroom along with that person. Her eyes widened in disbelief and shock as she opened her mouth to yell, the same hands shut her mouth close with his palms.

"Shush. It's me." Shehryaar's husky voice hits her hard. It made her feel things she wasn't supposed to be feeling. And to add his soft yet hard palms against her mouth, was something else entirely. She'd go berserk today. Leila was sure of that.

She tried to push him away and run but he was quicker than her, as he pushed her against the wall and placed his hands on either side; making sure she doesn't run away.He wanted answers from her and he'd get it, at any cost. Even if caging her like this was the only option left, he'd happily do it.

"What the hell is wrong with you?" She yelled at him whilst pushing his hands away. He placed them back again and looked into her hazel brown eyes.

She was now speechless at his actions. She averted her gaze not being able to look at his charcoal grey eyes. It was her most favourite pair of eyes in the whole damn world, but looking at them again after so long was making her go crazy. Beyond crazy if you ask her.

"Exactly I was wondering the same thing. What is wrong with me? You're driving me insane, Leila Qureshi." he yelled at her in frustration.

"What do you mean?" She angrily looks up at him and had to look into his beautiful eyes yet again. Why's it still a distraction to her? Was her genuine question which she was asking herself. Here she wants to stay mad and knock some sense to her stupid ex-fiancé and him being so damn handsome was starting to bother her very much.

His eyes though looked so hurt and broken but so were hers. They were both hurt and broken because of someone else's sick doings.

"What's wrong with me? Yeah, there's definitely something wrong. Tabhi I'm still not able to stop loving you even after everything you've done." Shehryaar whispered in a vulnerable voice as he chuckled dryly. She looked shocked at this new revelation. Being so close to her and staring deep into her hazel brown eyes was driving him insane but he tried his best to act sane.

"Stop joking Shehryaar, we both know how much you hate me," Leila muttered bitterly.

"Maybe that's true too. I do hate you, hate you so much for ruining us. Hate you so much for your guts to cheat on me and act so oblivion about it. Hate you so much for still making me feel things." He whispered in his dangerous voice whilst tracing her hair which fell on her face. She was taken aback at that. But her eyes became red in anger. His fingers itched to run his hands through her hair but it wasn't the right time nor was this conversation. But he wanted to do it anyway.

"Just move already. I don't have time for your rubbish." Leila muttered furiously as she tried to push him away but he held her more firmly.

"Let me go, Shehryaar." He smiled bitterly at that.

"I wish it was that easy."

"Why did you do that Leila? I th-tought you lo-oved me." Shehryaar whispered in his broken voice yet again. Any moment now, Leila was going to break down. She's sure of that.3

"I thought you loved me too. But I was wrong. If really did love me, then you would know I'm not like that." She replied with a sad smile on her face as fresh tears brimmed in her eyes. She couldn't see his face as her eyes were blurred with tears.

"Stop lying now, Leila. I saw you both with my own eyes." He so badly wanted to believe her but those images of her, unconscious on someone else bed in a dishevelled state refused to leave his mind. It still haunted him to date.

"It's a waste talking with you anyways. Just let me go already." Leila whispered in a sad voice. Shehryaar was hating this conversation with every passing second. He hated seeing her tears. His hands itched to wipe them away but he restrained himself from doing that.

"Just tell me why you did that. Please, Leila." She has had enough now. Pushing him away with force, Leila freed herself.

"I don't have to prove anything to you, Shehryaar Qureshi. Just stay away from me." He looked at her disappearing image with a frown on his face.

He should have done this earlier but it is better late than never. Picking up his phone, he dialled his friend; Arham Khan, who's a private investigator.

"Hello, Arham... I want your help with something."
***

It was the same night that day where everyone was gathered in the dining hall for dinner. Basheer Qureshi cleared his throat to gain everyone's attention. They all looked up at him curiously.

"I was thinking, along with Leila we should also conduct Shehryaar and Armeena's nikkah." Shehryaar froze at those words, he wondered from where did that come from

"But." Hamad wanted to deny this, he knew his son too well but was stopped by Agha Jaan himself who sternly added," it's decided and I'm not hearing no for an answer."

Bee Jaan looked at her husband in disbelief and so was everyone else. The only happy persons are Armeena and her family.

"I'm not marrying her or anyone else for that matter." Shehryaar too added firmly shocking his Agha Jaan to the core.3

"You're getting old, Shehryaar. You should get married soon. I wish to see my Great-grandchildren before I die." Agha Jaan was not letting him back off that easily. He was a stubborn man, but only Shehryaar had the guts to say no to him in this whole family.

"I don't care about that. I'm not marrying her and that's final. You can't force me, Agha Jaan. It's against the Islamic law." Shehryaar muttered with an eye roll as he got up from the dining table and left the place making everyone gasp at the scene.

Armeena has never been so humiliated in her whole life, she was on the verge of breaking down.

Leila was not sure how to react to this. Sure she had expected something like that from her dear Agha Jaan but Shehryaar's reaction has surprised her very much.

Giving Armeena the same smug smile which she gave her in the morning, Leila continued to eat her dinner. She was the only person in there to think about food when the atmosphere around them was so tensed. She couldn't care less. Food was more important anyway

Agha Jaan and Armeena fumed in frustration and anger, maybe they did succeed in separating Shehryaar and Leila but their plan of getting him married to Armeena was a big-time fail.
Karma was a bitch after all.

The people who are meant to be in your life will always gravitate towards you, no matter how far they wander.

# FOUR
## CHAPTER 04

Nothing can separate you from the people who are meant to be in your life. They will always come back.

***

Betrayal is probably the worst ever feeling especially when; it's your family who betrayed you.

Shehryaar couldn't fathom that his Agha Jaan could have stooped so low as to trash someone's name just so that he wouldn't marry her. It was something that he's finding hard to digest. But it was the truth. He has been used and lied by his own grandfather and he felt like such a fool all along.

Guilt was far from what he is feeling right now. Words couldn't describe his feelings and to think how Leila must have gone through all of this alone, has hit him so hard. He has been blaming her for cheating on him for over a year when it's him who cheated her, he has promised to not leave her no matter what and took the first step ahead to walk away when a problem came.

What he didn't understand was his grandfather; Why'd he do that? Isn't Leila his granddaughter too?2

Shehryaar needed answers and he was going to get them. Taking long strides towards Agha Jaan's room, he paused at his bedroom door and before he could enter, he saw Armeena and Agha Jaan indulged in a deep conversation, their backs faced him. They had no idea of his presence until now.

"Don't worry, Meena. I'll get you married with Shehryaar and it's my promise to you."

"He still loves her, Agha Jaan. That's the only reason why Shehryaar denied to marry me." Bawling her eyes out, Armeena complaints angrily.

"So? Love is not everything. I'm letting my grandson to marry an illegitimate woman. I stopped their marriage once and I will do it again too." Shehryaar gasped at this revelation. He stood there frozen to his spot, as Armeena complaints all about her efforts to make him notice her, who paid zero attention to her.9

Basheer Qureshi was a man of principles. He followed them all his life and didn't like it when someone doesn't agree with his points of view. He had three sons and a daughter. Yes, a daughter which they never spoke of, for over two decades.

He never liked to talk about his daughter, that got pregnant before marriage and refused to abort her child. Basheer literally begged her for an abortion, but Sadiya Qureshi was as stubborn as her father and never gave in. She never revealed who the baby's father was until her last breath making it all complicated. She died while giving birth to the baby.

Basher didn't shed a single tear on her death, all he could think of was that baby, which could tarnish his family's name in society and he wanted to get rid of that baby as fast as he could. All his dreams were shattered when his second son, Faik decided to adopt that misfortune of a baby which took his daughter's life away. He never liked Leila before nor will he ever like her.3

He went berserk when Shehryaar announced his likings towards her, wanting to marry Leila. How can he let that happen now? What will happen to his Qureshi heir? He can't let some illegitimate woman carry the next heir of the Qureshi's. It would happen over his dead body or so he thought. He even successfully stopped the marriage but what he couldn't succeed was getting Shehryaar married to someone of his choice.

It didn't take rocket science to connect the dots for Shehryaar. Maybe that's why, his grandfather was too eager to get Leila married off quickly so that he forgets her and marries someone else, someone legitimate? What a sick man. He thought with a frown.

Armeena wiped away her tears as she got assured that Shehryaar would be hers, no matter what. When she turned around to leave the room, she got the shock of her life. Her eyes widened and her legs froze.

"Sheh-hryaar." Hearing Armeena's stuttering, Basheer Qureshi turns around and he himself was shocked.

"I'm ashamed to call you both my family," Shehryaar muttered in disbelief and disgust.

Before they could defend themselves for their sick actions, he marched away from there angrily.

Talking with them was a waste of time anyway and he had far better things to do. For instance mending his broken relationship, which he knew is going to be hard. But Shehryaar vowed to not give up so easily.

He'd redeem his mistakes and beg for her forgiveness even if it takes all his life, he'd just do that if it gets him to be with her at the end. He'd do that without a care in the world.

God, he was such a fool. How could fall he on their traps?
***

Leila couldn't think straight ever since her conversation with Shehryaar in the storeroom. She couldn't sleep the whole night. He still loved her. That's what he told. And it is freaking her out because his eyes looked straight into hers when he said those words. It has to be the truth because when he lies he won't meet your eyes, that much she knows about him.

But what's the use of loving someone when you cannot believe them in their vulnerable times?

Leila was so mad. Mad at him for making her cry like this. Mad at him for what he did. So mad at him for still having this effect on her.

She hates him. Period

But at the same time, she'd be lying if she told that she stopped loving him because it never happened. She couldn't get herself to do that. Unloving him was something so hard. Both for him and her.

She loved him yeah but hated him too. Shehryaar confused her stupid heart.

Luckily it was a Sunday, so she didn't have to make any excuses for not going to college. Honestly, she was so done. So done with everything.

Leila stared at his figure with a blank face whilst wiping her tears, she must have really lost her mind because she even started imagining about him. But the blank look disappears as soon as she realized it wasn't any imagination and he was there for real.

"What the hell are you doing here?" She asked startled by his unexpected visit. He never stepped into the west wing, let alone her room. Did he get hit somewhere on his head, she wondered with a frown.

Becoming a little self-conscious, she covered herself properly with a shawl and glared at him for an explanation. He sat down on his knees just beside her, startling her yet again.

"Le-leila..." Her name came out as a mere whisper. Shehryaar felt so ashamed to be here, in front of her. Her glare turns into confusion as soon as she hears that soft and broken voice of his.

What shocked her next was his pale face and teary eyes. Wait a minute... Is he crying? She gasped at the person in front of her.

Shehryaar Qureshi was the most strong person she has ever come across and crying is a very big deal when it was him.

Her hands ached to grab his handsome face and wipe off the tears but she stopped herself from doing anything stupid like that.

"What happened to you?" She asked with genuine concern. He was taken aback at that. God, she was so pure. She was concerned about him when in reality she should be hating him. He lost such a gem. How could he ever doubt her?

"I'm sorry." It came out as a mere whisper.

"What for? She opened her mouth to ask but stopped herself when the realization hits her.

"Took you long enough." She muttered coldly, long gone was her concern. Shehryaar has expected this and a lot more. But he's not going to give up if that's what she wants.

"You didn't explain." was his only excuse and she scoffed at that.

"And you thought that I could do something as low as that? Just because my birth mom did that doesn't mean I'm like her too. How could you all think so low of me." Leila cried in anger. She was so mad at her grandfather for setting this upon her. He made it clear that he won't let her marry him and he happily succeeded in that. She never told it to anyone because she has trusted their love and in the end, it was she who got fooled.

If not for her parents, who had an abundance of belief and trust upon her, she'd be on the roads by now. That's what Agha Jaan wanted too. But bless her parents. They didn't let their eyes fool their belief in their daughter. They trusted her, period.

That's what she has expected from Shehryaar too. But too many expectations always ends up hurting us and it did with her too.

"I don't have any explanation for this Leila. I believed what my eyes saw and you didn't bother to explain anything. You just left. It was as if our relationship was not important at all." Shehryaar held her hands but she jerked it away with a frown.

"So you're blaming me now?" She shrieked in anger.

"Can you blame me for believing what I saw? Imagine walking into a man's room and finding your finance who'd become your wife in two freaking days in that situation? Can you really blame me? I was just another insecure man at that time Leila. I was so mad at you... And tell me what would you do if I were in your position?" Shehryaar cross-questioned her and she had no response for that.

She was speechless.

"I know what I did was a mistake, I should have trusted you more than anyone else. But I'm sorry okay. I'd do anything to get your forgiveness. But just so you know, you're mistaken in this too." He muttered weakly. She didn't understand where all of this was going. He continued with his rants.

"Whatever it was, I deserved an honest explanation. If I didn't believe you after that, maybe then I'd be wrong. But you never explained. Which ultimately told me that you are wrong and I hated you all along."

"Would it have changed anything, if I explained it to you?" She asked dryly. Somewhere deep down, Leila has realised her mistake too.3

"God, Leila. It would have changed so many things." He held her hands again, his knees hurt but he stayed in that position. She didn't pull away this time.

God, it felt so good to just hold her hands like this. He has missed it. Missed everything about her.

"What do we do now?" She asked in a low whisper. Leila was too shocked to remain sane, all of this which are happening way beyond her imagination and she feared if she wakes up, it will end up being a dream. She didn't want it to be a dream. She wanted this to be real. She wanted him to be sorry for what he did.

"What will it take for you to forgive me?" He asked her with hopeful eyes. She had no answer to that. Did he plan on making her speechless all the time or what?

"Honestly, I don't know."

"I didn't lie when I said, I love you yesterday. Because I still do, after everything that has happened I still love you. My heart couldn't unlove you. It still beats for you. Only you." He whispered with a sad smile.

All she could do was nod her head, "I know" she mouthed whilst fighting away the tears.

"Please tell me honestly, Leila. Do you also love me? I understand if you don't. But I need your answer. This could change our whole life." Shehryaar asked her. She stared at him wide-eyed. She couldn't stop her tears this time, which he wiped away slowly. And God, all she wanted to do was throw her arms around him and hug him tightly. How much has she missed that sweet little gestures of his.

"Yes or no?" He asked again.

"Yes." She meekly replied.

She never stopped. Even after everything. It was a tough job to stop loving someone when all your heart wants was that person.

A beam formed on his face as he heard those words. She still loved him. Even after all the happenings she still loved. How did he get so lucky?

"But what will that have to do with anything!? It doesn't change anything." Leila replied with a sad smile. Her eyes looked hurt and broken as she said those words. He was offended at that.

"It has many things to do with."

Puzzled by his blank statement she questioned," what do you mean?"

"For instance, I want to be with you, it is as simple and as complicated as that." She jerked away her hands from his hold and glared at him.

"That's not happening."

"But I want it to happen, Leila. I so badly want it to happen. Please think about it... A second chance. We need a second chance because life was cruel during the first time and we deserve better. We were both wronged and played on. I want us to have a second chance, Leila. Please." Leila has never seen him so vulnerable before.

But a second chance, should she really give him that?

The timing isn't always right, but eventually destiny steps in. All you need is patience.

# FIVE

## CHAPTER 05

There's never a reason not to chase the ones who make you feel something.

***

Time. Leila wanted time to decide whether or not she'd want to give him a second chance. Shehryaar agreed to it but he is getting impatient with every passing day, it's been two weeks now. She has been avoiding him like a plague. He decided to get into action so that she would agree to the second chance, he really wanted to prove to her that the second chance would be worth it. So worth it.

It was one of those days, where Leila was late for her college; nothing unusual and a smirk appears on his face as he thought of a plan. Taking out his phone, he messaged all of his drivers and asked them to take the car for service, immediately. Leila has been eating her breakfast silently, with her head glued towards the plate. Not once did she dare to look up into his beautiful charcoal eyes. She was aware of his staring, it happened a lot these days. But Leila decided to act oblivion about it

How easy it is for him to come and ask sorry, expecting her to forgive him just like that. She was a human too and she needed time to make her heart understand that all of this was happening in real. She still couldn't believe that Shehryaar has apologised for his actions. She never dreamt of this day. But it came anyway. And now she's clueless about what to do further.

After gulping a glass of water, Leila got up from her seat. Shehryaar watched her disappearing image with a sly smile. After a minute, he too gets out of there and when he came out he was shocked for a second.

Leila smiled at the red roses and the note attached to them, which read; Is your name Google? Because you got everything I'm searching for. Inhaling the fragrance of rose, she smiled again.

It had no name on it, so she has assumed that it was Shehryaar. But what she didn't expect was to see him marching towards her with a frown on his face.

"Who gave this to you?" He asked her angrily, his eyes fumed with rage and possessiveness.

Confused, Leila frowned upon his question," what do you mean who gave this? I thought it was you."

Shehryaar snatched the roses from her hands and then read the note, he couldn't help but cringe at it.

"You think I'd do something as stupid as this?" He grimaced at that thought. She scrunched her nose and walked around hoping to find her car so that she'd get away with this. She had no idea who has sent her that but if any more minute passes, Shehryaar might lose his cool. That much she knows about him. But as far as her eyes could go, their big parking lot was empty and there was only a single car; which was Shehryaar's.

"Where are the cars?" Turning around, angrily she questioned him. She knew it was him. A smirk appears on his face as he strides towards her. After crushing the roses under his shoes.

'Oh, the poor rose.' Leila thought with a frown.

"You answer me first, who gave that to you?" He asked her again as he eyed that crushed roses.

"Seriously? I don't know." Leila answered honestly but a smirk appears on her face as she guessed who it was. That could be the only possibility.

"It must be Junaid. My future husband." Shehryaar's face was so worth watching, she tried hard not to laugh. His eyes became red in fury. Anymore second, she'd burst out laughing. But Leila was caught off guard as he pulled her wrists and twisted them from behind, pulling her close to him. It made her hit on his chest. She gasped at this sudden closeness. Her bag fell off her hands in the process.8

Breathe in. Breathe out.

Shehryaar closed his eyes to control himself. Leila looked at his face with a confused and innocent look on her face.

"I know I have been a big jerk to you, Leila." He muttered weakly whilst opening his eyes.1

"But don't ever talk about getting married to someone else. Because that is not happening. You're my Leila. Just mine." He whispered huskily into her eyes, making her shiver under his breath against her earlobes.

"What about my marriage? They've already fixed it I believe." Mischievously she asked him that, his face screamed the words; anger and frustration. But it was so fun to pull his legs.

"To hell with it. Remember this always, you're my Leila. Shehryaar's Leila. Always have and always will be." Shehryaar muttered possessively as he cupped her cheeks, gently.

Leila shut her eyes at his words. The stupid man still had that stupid effect on her even after all these years.

"Am I clear?" He asked again. She opened her eyes and looked into his. Even though his voice was dangerous and possessive, his eyes screamed otherwise. It looked so vulnerable and scared. He was scared of losing her to someone else and it is eating him alive.

"Please don't leave me, Leila. I'm broken without you." Not hearing any reply from her, he finally showed her his weakness. She was his weakness and a life without her seemed like hell to him. He'd do anything just to have her back in his life, anything.

"I was broken without you too. You broke me so much, cherry." Shehryaar's eyes beamed at his nickname. He has heard that one after a year now. Nostalgia hits him hard.

"I'm sorry is all I have to say. Please forgive me, Leila. I'll do anything to get you back. Tell me what." Shehryaar asked as he tucked her hair strands behind her ears. All this while, he has been holding her like this, close to him.

"I know you're sorry. But I'm scared okay. What if something else happens again? I can't help but think that you'd leave me again." Leila expressed her insecurity openly. He gaped at those words.

"I'd not do that, you know right?"

"It's your actions which made me think like that," Leila muttered whilst trying to pull away from his grip. But he held her more firmly.

"I'd never repeat the same mistake again, Leila. I know asking you to trust me is stupid. But do you forgive me?" He asked her with a hopeful voice.

"I-i do." She replied with a small smile on her face. Relief washed over his heart as he heard those words.

"Don't you think that we both deserve a second chance?" this time his voice was calm and composed. She looked into his eyes whilst blinking in yes. He has never felt so happy before, not even when they got engaged he was this happy. What he felt now was far from being just happy. It was entirely something else.

"The things you do to me, Leila Qureshi." Inhaling her sweet fragrance he whispered those words making her shiver under his presence.

"I missed you." She said with teary eyes, wiping away those tears he replied, "I missed you more."

"You're such a liar." Huffing angrily, Leila pulled away from his grip.

"Janaan. I'm not lying. I seriously missed you." He caught her wrists again with a chuckle. A blush crept onto her cheeks at his endearment. It was his favourite endearment which he used for her in the past.1

"But on a serious note, will you marry me?" Trust him to be so brutally blunt like that. Leila froze at his words.9

"Marr-ry y-you?"

"Yes, marry me... So that I can kiss you with all my might."

Just remember that some people will be worth a second chance

# SIX
# CHAPTER 06

Forgiving is easy, but forgetting is not.

...

Shehryaar has loved Leila for as long as he could remember. Even when they drifted apart from each other, due to that huge misunderstanding, he still loved her. It was impossible for him to stop loving her. Even if he denied it a hundred times, deep down only he knew how painful it was for him to watch her every freaking day and not talk with her, make fun of her or laugh along with her. It hurt him so much and he wouldn't deny he hated her for it. He hated her so much.

But he was ready to forgive her and take her back in a blink of an eye if only she came and apologized for what she did. That day never came. They both gave their egos the first priority and stopped seeing each other's face, how much ever frustrating it was. Their pride didn't let them take the first step.

Neither did Shehryaar thought about it deeply nor did Leila gave him the proper explanation which he deserved to get. Both of them were right and wrong in their own places, but mostly it was the ego that won at the end.

Now when he realized what the actual truth was, things took a drastic turn.

"Marry you?" Giving him a sarcastic laugh Leila pulled away from his grip. He gave her a confused stare. His cheesy statement did not even affect her as much. All she could process was the word, marriage and her mind was blank all over again.

"Yeah, sure. What's the guarantee that you won't leave me once again?" Leila shot him a furious glare. The word marriage does things to her heart, which she hasn't shared with anyone before.

No one would understand her feelings unless their supposed lover rejected them just two days before the actual wedding.

"You said you forgave me?" Shehryaar asked blankly, he was so elated just a moment ago and now hearing her say this made him restless.

"Forgiven. Not forgotten. I've never forgotten the hurt you gave me, Shehryaar. You hurt me so damn much and suddenly you cannot just come back in my life and marry me." She snapped at him in fury.

Of course. What else did he expect?

"You hurt me too, Leila. You hurt me so much. I'm mistaken, I agree... but partly it was your mistake too. You did not even explain me. What did you expect from me after seeing such a scene with my own eyes." Shehryaar replied angrily.

He was so frustrated with her at this point. They were fine just a moment ago and now this.

"I know and I'm not going to justify my actions. I do forgive you, but I'm not ready for the marriage yet. A second chance yes. But not so soon. The humiliation once faced was more than enough." She cried in anger while refusing to look into his eyes, forcibly he held her shoulders and made her look at him.

"Please stop crying, Leila. I'm sorry. I'd do anything to get your forgiveness. To get you back in my life... Just say." Shehryaar asked in a pleading voice as he wiped away her tears, she slowly gazed into his beautiful charcoal eyes and lost her senses for a while.

"I forgave you. But do understand that I'm scared. I cannot just forget everything and come back to you... We both deserve a second chance, I agree. But I'm unsure of this relationship. I'm going crazy thinking that things might end in misery once again."

"It won't." He said whilst cupping her cheeks.

"I need space." Leila pulled back once again. He looked hurt by her actions but it was getting too much for her to handle. All she wanted to do was to say yes and marry him but God should only help her. She's so scared. Scared of all the what-ifs.

Hurt by her actions, Shehryaar maintained some distance from her. She gave him an apologetic stare.

"You said you'd give us a second chance?" He asked her with hopeful eyes.

"I did." She never declined that.

"Then why won't you marry me?" This girl, she's the only one who can make him feel so many things at the same time.

"I wish it was that easy." Leila chuckled nervously.

Their moment gets interrupted with a loud honk, startling both of them. Snapping their head in confusion; they found a car parking in front of them.

"Are they Khaled's?" Shehryaar asked in astonishment. Leila wished it was a dream or something but only it wasn't.

"Why do they look like they're going to burst into flames or something?" Leila whispered to him in a low voice, he couldn't disagree with that. The Mother and father of Junaid did look very angry.

Still confused, Leila passed them a polite smile as she looked at them both. But they didn't return it rather they frowned at her.

Shehryaar was taken aback at that. Just two weeks ago, they were going crazy about Leila and now they were frowning at her. Was it for real!?, He wondered in confusion.

Ignoring them both like they never existed, Zara Khaled and her husband marched into the villa.

Passing curious glances towards each other, Leila and Shehryaar entered their villa, silently.

Long forgotten was her bag, which fell down over there and their heated conversation which they've just shared.2

Humera was confused when she saw her daughter's supposed in-laws come to their home unannounced. Panic overtook her heart, as she sat across them. She did not even bother to ask why Leila hasn't gone to college yet, she saw her leave with her own eyes but that was not important now.

They passed each other greetings and the Khaled's looked at each other sceptically.

"We are sorry, Mrs Qureshi… but we're calling off this wedding," Zara muttered those words, not feeling sorry at all.

"What?" Humera exclaimed in horror, Leila snapped her head at that.

The only happy person was Shehryaar.

"Don't give that surprised look, Mrs Qureshi. Why didn't you tell us beforehand about your daughter's doings? Such an ugly character behind that pretty face. What did you all take us for?" Zara muttered angrily.

Tears formed in Leila's eyes, as she heard those words. She understood why are they calling off the wedding.

"We can explain… It's a misunderstanding." Humera tried to pacify them while Leila sat there numbly.

"What misunderstanding? When her own cousin refused to marry her. Then why would my son become the scapegoat?"

"ENOUGH NOW." Shehryaar who could not tolerate tears in Leila's eyes yelled at that lady in anger. She flinched in fear.

"You don't want your son to marry her? Great. You should just leave... Not another word against her and yes ask your son to not send any more roses to her." Huffing angrily, the old couple left the Qureshi villa, for good.

Humera was confused about everything.

"You knew?" She asked her nephew sceptically. He nodded his head in shame, and couldn't even look at her face.

"How?" Humera asked.

"It was Agha Jaan who set her up," Shehryaar muttered those words bitterly. Humera's eyes widened at that. She knew that her father in law hated her daughter, but to this extent, she had no idea.

"Leila..." Calling her name softly, he held her hands.

Humera watched her kids with a sad smile on her face. They were both so broken and hurt for no fault of theirs. They both did not deserve that.

"Leila, say something." Shehryaar was hating how much aloof Leila was looking. She used to be so lively and bubbly once upon a time.

Not having anything to say, Leila yanked her hands and ran away from there.

Shehryaar watched the disappearing figure of her with a gloomy look on his face. He understood that she has forgiven him but to forget everything she needed time. He broke her trust and was paying its cost now.

Maybe it's not always about trying to fix something that is broken. Maybe it's about starting over and create something better.

# SEVEN
## CHAPTER 07

Life is a balance of holding on and letting go.
***

Faik and Humera were so disappointed when they learnt that it was Agha Jaan, because of whom all the chaos has taken place in their children's lives. They didn't realize that a person could stoop so low as to do something as cheap as that until Basheer Qureshi has proved them wrong.

"Why didn't you tell us earlier, Leila?" Faik asked his daughter with a frown, he was seriously regretting not digging the matters deeper, if not for the promise he has made to her, then he'd have definitely found out who has dared to do such things to his only daughter.

"I knew you all would hate him and there would be such a big rift in the families, I just know." Leila cried in her mother's arms, who stroked her hair lovingly; trying to pacify her daughter.

"He didn't deserve to be loved anyway, I'm ashamed that he's my father," Faik muttered in a disgust filled voice.

Leila didn't have anything to say after that. She knew that things would get worse if they came to know about the reality. She didn't want to be the reason for wreaking such a big family and begged her father to let that matter go, he gave up as she swore on her life and took that damn promise from him.

"I don't want to talk about that horrifying day anymore. I want to let it go, let everything go so that I can start afresh, please ammi and abbu, we are not going to make any fuss out of this, okay?" Leila asked as she glanced at both of them with tired eyes. They nodded in agreement and after that day, nobody ever spoke of that night.

Days passed in a blur and just like that Leila has now graduated with her master's degree. No one in the family spoke with Basheer Qureshi anymore and slowly he stopped coming out of his room. His own wife was so disgusted by his actions that she sleeps in the guest room. The family was now back to how they used to be a year ago when all of this nonsense didn't take place. They were happy. Alhamdulillah!

Sheryaar and Leila had a silent agreement of taking things slow.

He respected her opinions and gave her the space that she wanted. But he didn't just fade away, he stayed around this time. Subtly stuck with her to prove that he won't be leaving her anytime soon. He used to always try and get her into any type of conversation with him. At first, it was awkward but things changed slowly. He even gifted her a cat on her twenty-second birthday as a sorry-for-everything type of gift and she could swear that it was the best ever gift. She loved cats and he was so using that. He did everything in him to woo her back, Leila did notice all of that and honestly, it was all she needed. To be assured that he wouldn't leave her and his every action was melting her like butter.

It was true that he didn't trust her, enough. Nor did she gave him a valid explanation. But nothing could be changed about that and they let it go. Mistakes were a part of a human anyway.

Slowly but steadily she has begun to warm up to him. They now talk with each other without that damn discomfort lingering in some corner and it was such a big process that everyone noticed. The elders were so happy for them both and all they ever pray was for Leila and Shehryaar to be happy again. In all the chaos, it was them who suffered the most for no fault of theirs and they both deserved nothing but happiness.

It was just another lazy day for Leila as she sat in the living room and munched on her favourite pakora, prepared by her ammi dearest. She has taken a year gap to take some much-needed rest and then she'd join in some job, that's what she has planned.

"Assalamualaikum." her head snapped at the tired voice of Shehryaar and a smile tugged at her lips involuntarily.

"Walaikum Aslam, busy day?" standing up from the sofa, she came forward whilst picking the mug of water and came towards him; who lazily fell on the sofa opposite to the one which she sat. Looking at the water in her hands, Shehryaar smiled gladly as he took it from her and gulped it in a go.

"I'll get that favourite tea of yours," Leila mumbled to herself as she ran towards the kitchen, and he couldn't help but smile like some creep.

Bee Jaan who walked through that way smiled to herself as she witnessed the scene and a thought comes to her mind, grinning ear to ear she goes into her room and asked her helper to call her sons and daughters-in-law into the room.

It was high time that she set things right. Shehryaar and Leila were hopeless anyways.

***

Unannounced guests always came with surprises. The Qureshi's were so not expecting the Aziz family to visit them all of a sudden. Kasim Aziz was the cousin brother of Sara Qureshi; Sherhryaar's mother and she was as surprised as everyone else in her family upon their unexpected visit.

The Aziz family consisted of, Kasim and his wife Isha, and their two children Ayesha and Arhan. They were twins and a dangerous one at that. They loved pranking everyone and nobody wishes to get on their bad side. Even at twenty-four years old, they still behaved childishly at times. And their parents thought that it was high time to get them both married, so they'd learn to grow up a little bit. Leila was glad that the annoying twins didn't visit along with their parents.

"I know you all are surprised by our visit, we did have our reasons." Kasim nervously smiled as he kept the teacup aside, his wife smiled as well.

"We don't like to beat around the bushes, no one likes them anyway. I came here to ask your Shehryaar and Leila's hand for our Ayesha and Arhan." there was pin-drop silence after that. None of the Qureshi's was able to utter any word.2

Armeena felt herself burning in rage as she abruptly left the place, with her parents trailing behind her. At times they all did forget her existence and it hurt her a lot. Every time it was only Leila and Shehryaar, it was like nobody cared for her.

"Did we say something wrong?" Isha asked apologetically. The Qureshi's still didn't know how to react, yet.

It was Faik who broke the silence," we need time, Kasim Bhai. All of this is so sudden and unexpected. And it is our children' life we are talking about."

"Of course, take all the time you want. I hope for a positive answer though." Kasim smiled happily.

During the whole damn time, there were those two eyes that couldn't blink away from each other. Shehryaar had to gulp his saliva as he stared at her hazel brown eyes from afar, she stared right back at him. Their eyes spoke a million things which their mouths could never speak.

There was this sudden fear, fear of losing each other one more time and that too for real this time. Just the mere thought of it has pained their hearts. The thought of seeing him/ her with someone else made them both so vulnerable and scared.

And that fear was so visible in both of their eyes. Leila tried hard to fight away that tears, why was she getting so weak? She had no idea but the thought of getting married to someone else was making her lose her shit.

NO... Shehryaar wanted to yell in front of everyone and make things clear to them that he's not marrying anyone nor will he allow his Leila to marry anyone else for that matter. But he controlled himself for the reputation and respect his family's name had. And he wouldn't be too foolish to tarnish that by reacting in such a way. It took a lot for him to control himself, but he did it anyway.

***

Leila was pacing back and forth in her room as she recollected the morning's incident again and again. She refused to get out of her room ever since. The thought of Shehryaar marrying someone else was driving her insane and she didn't know what to do anymore. And there was no way that she's marrying that Arhan.1

But... She was so very scared. Scared of the thought that her Shehryaar will marry someone else and forget all about her. Of course, she was crazy to think like that but there was still a possibility. She did push him away when he wanted her back in his life and now she's starting to question herself; what did she really want?1

To be with Shehryaar or to be away with him?

But there was something which she didn't need to think that much anyway. Leila could never be able to see him with someone else, especially not that Ayesha and that proved her to be as possessive as him. And it shook her from within.

Her chain of thoughts breaks down as she heard her door click open and there was only one person who'd dare to do that kind of stuff. She stood frozen to her spot, suddenly as he intensely stared at her. She blinked, twice. And he was still there.

Definitely not an imagination. Her inner self mocked at her.

"I don't want you to marry him."

"I don't want you to marry her." they both blurted out at the same and were surprised at that coincidence. Their eyes locked with each other once again and the whole world seemed to freeze.3

Shehryaar and Leila sure had their fair share of differences and misunderstandings, but they'd not let go of each other that easily. It wouldn't happen, not in this lifetime at least.

And suddenly you know it's time to start something new and trust the magic of new beginnings.

# EIGHT
## CHAPTER 08

It's never too late to live happily ever after.

***

The Aziz family were certainly disappointed when they learned the answer to the proposal, which was a no. They really did hope for a positive answer but they should have guessed it already with the way Leila and Shehryaar stared at each other when the question of marriage was raised. It's been a day now. The Qureshi family has been surprisingly planning something behind their children's back and they were more than happy when Shehryaar asked for permission to take Leila out that day.

And now, the loud honking of cars from behind made Leila frown, why can't these people ever that just because they honk we can't move forward. It's the signal which controls all. Shehryaar chuckled at her face which he found rather funny. She has been inpatient throughout the ride, not knowing where she was taken to has made her frustrated, to say the least.

"Where?" she began but was cut off by him again, who added," do you trust me?"

She became blank at once.

"Don't answer that." fearing that her answer would be no, he quickly looked away. Gaining back her trust was the next difficult thing but he did try.

"I d-do." Leila didn't dare look at his face nor his eyes as she blurted those words. His charcoal grey eyes widened in surprise as he stared at her. She had her face averted from him. Luckily the signal was still on the red lights, so he could spare some time to make her look at him.

"Did you really say that?" she nodded her head sceptically, it took a lot in her to trust him again, all she could hope was for him to not break it again.

"I tru-st you." she said again as he looked in her eyes, her lashes blinked innocently making her look so beautiful and tempting, it took everything in him to not grab that gorgeous face of hers and kiss her. It was wrong, they weren't married yet. But they will soon and he's planning to take revenge for every time she has tested his self-control. It's going to be very sweet revenge, of course.

"Thank you,"Shehryaar replied her with a grin as he started the car again when the signal became green again. All the while Leila had her head glued to the window as she stared outside at the busy roads of Hyderabad.

"Exactly where are we?" Leila was confused as to why they have parked in front of the hospital, she was worried now. The thought of something happening to her closed ones shook her from within.

"Get down, first," he replied softly whilst opening the door for her. And when he saw her sitting still, gave her his hands instead which she held tightly as she got down.

"You will definitely be surprised. But in the end, it's going to be worth it. Insha Allah." he whispered softly, confusing her further as they both walked ahead.

Leila who was scared held his hand tighter, as they entered some special ward. Her eyes fell on one man, who was lying lifelessly on the hospital bed," who is he?" she asked him impatiently, but he shushed her as the man on the bed opened his eyes slowly.

"L-eila... You came." words were difficult for him to form but he spoke anyway, she was confused as to how this person knew her name but Shehryaar nodded his head assuringly making her a little relaxed.

"Who are you?" she asked the person, directly, who had a sad smile on his face as soon as he heard that question.

With great difficulty he removed his oxygen mask and sat up," I pray that no other father in this world should get asked this question from his daughter." her eyes widened in both surprise and shock. Her legs felt too weak to stand anymore, if not for Shehryaar holding her hand, she might have fallen down.

"Yo-u-you- are ly-ing." she blinked away her tears, not wanting to believe any of this.

"I'm sorry, my dear. I had no other way to keep you safe, I had to sacrifice you to keep you alive," he replied in a low voice. She gave him a puzzled look.

"I don't believe you," she replied firmly. This can't be, right?

"He's not lying, Leila." Shehryaar blinked his eyes at her shocked face. Tears rolled down her cheeks continuously as soon as she heard those words.

"Why did you hate me so much?" Leila asked coldly yet her voice showed how vulnerable she was.

"I and your mother fell in love with you, even before you were born Leila, trust me. I never hated you." she looked at the person in front of her, her real father more clearly this time. Only then she realized why she never resembled her birth mom because she was a replica of her dad and that made her cry harder.

"Why did you do this to me?" It wasn't like Leila hated its results, she at least got Faik and Humera as her parents through that and that was such a big blessing. It was just that she wanted answers and she deserved to get them.

"First of all, you're not an illegitimate child. Don't let anyone tell you otherwise." the man said in a serious tone, taking Leila by surprise yet again.

"You're the legal child of Farooq and his wife, Sadiya Farooq Khan." Shehryaar held her hands tighter with this new revelation. She was looking like she'd pass out any moment soon.

"When I knew that keeping you with me would risk your precious life, I gave you to my best friend Faik, who promised to take care of you for me." he then explained to them of his family who belonged to the undercover world and how their enemies have targeted and killed every single member of his family except him. Leila was shocked would be an understatement.

"I know this isn't a proper excuse. But I had no other choice, my dear." the old man exclaimed helplessly.

"Why didn't no one knew about your and Sadiya ammi's marriage?"

"I was protecting her by hiding that marriage but a person will have to die if that's what the Almighty wants and she had to leave one day... She gave me this beautiful gift though, which I failed to take care of." he sadly smiled at Leila. That explained why Sadiya never disclosed who her child's father was. Everything made sense now and Leila was glad. Glad to know the actual truth.

"For what's worth, I'm sorry, beta. I'm truly very sorry." he asked her forgiveness and she nodded her head with a smile," I forgive you." those words meant the word to Farooq and he silently thanked Shehryaar for making all of this happen through his eyes. If not for him, this day would have never come. And the next half an hour went on emotionally with the duo catching up for all their lost years. Leila and Shehryaar left only after promising to visit him again.

***

"I'm not illegitimate." Leila grinned ear to ear as she smiled at Shehryaar, who nodded his head with a chuckle. He knew important it is for her to hear those words. She has been deeply affected by her Agha Jaan and his mindless words and now nothing can affect her anymore for it is going to lose its meaning.

She felt happy that her mother was not what everyone taunted her to be. She had Shehryaar to thank for that. If not for him, her whole life people must be taunting her mother for no-fault and it made her smile. Smile in happiness.

They were currently seated in one fancy restaurant as, by the time they came out of the hospital, it was time for dinner already.

"Leila..." Shehryaar called her name nervously.

She raised her brows in response.

"I do not want to beat around the bushes..." trailing off sceptically he continued," I don't think that there's any more power left in me to wait... I want to make you mine as soon as I can before something else happens and you leave me again. I want you to be my wife, Leila...Will you give that honour to me?" he asked whilst holding both her hands in his.

Her eyes went wide and her cheeks turned red.

She had been thinking about a lot lately, about the second chance which he wanted her to give. She did wanted this. All of this. Of course the fear of something breaking them apart, again was still there, it will be too much heartbreak when it happens all over again. But Leila was willing to take that risk. Now, what's life without some little bit of risks and hurdles?

"I'm shitting my pants here. Please tell me quickly..." he muttered anxiously making her chuckle. A blush crept onto her cheeks as she nodded her head in positive.

A big beam appears on his face, "Is that a yes?" she nodded her head shyly again.

"Words, Leila. Words," he demanded her like a child who wanted his candy.

"Y-yes... I will ma-marry y-you." she stuttered shyly whilst lowering her gaze, unable to meet his intense-looking ones. He was making her blush for no real reason, lately.

"Damn. I feel so happy." Shehryaar exclaimed happily whilst holding her hands tight in his, she looked up at him shyly. He really looked so happy. She has never seen him this happy before, maybe on that day when she forgave him, he was as happy. But today he looked a bit extra happy and why not? He was finally going to get the love of his life after all. It has been such a long wait. But in the end, it was so worth it.

and so the adventure begins.

# The End

Maybe it won't work out, but seeing if it does will be the best adventure ever.
***

Shehryaar's room has always been off-limits for Leila and so was her room to him, but that never stopped him from entering her room earlier, but she has strictly obeyed the rules though and now sitting in his room, on his bed, as his bride was making her blush crimson. Leila fidgeted with her fingers, as she waited for her husband to come in. The word husband hits her hard, and damn it still feels so freaking unbelievable.

His room was beautiful though, his bed was softer than hers and she fell in love with it almost instantly.

As soon as she heard the noise of the doorknob, clicking slowly; her heart began to beat faster than usual. She didn't dare look up at him as he took slow steps towards her and she could swear if he comes any closer her heart might jump out already. But it didn't, not when he sat just beside her, their legs touching, his hands came to lift the veil and she shut her eyes in shyness.

"The things you do to me, Leila Shehryaar Quereshi," he whispered dreamily whilst lazily removing the veil from her head, leaving her in a blouse and skirt along with some jewels. She still had her eyes shut taking everything in him to control himself. There's no stopping him today though.

Leila shivered whilst breathing unevenly as his hands came towards her neck which roamed from behind and in a swift he removed her necklace. She gasped in shock when his cold lips came in contact with her cheeks, she opened her eyes at once and met with her husband's beautiful charcoal grey eyes, which was ogling at her with love, burning desire and want.

"You look beautiful, Masha Allah." he kissed her forehead with love, making her blush hard if that was possible.

"Wait here, I'll come in a second."

Confused, Leila watched him walk to his wardrobe and taking out a box, with a mischievous grin, he came towards her. Taking his seat beside her once again, he placed the box in her hands, who raised her head in confusion.

"Your mooh dikhai gift." grinning at him, Leila opened the box and was in awe the moment her eyes fell on the most gorgeous diamond bracelet she has ever seen.

"I take it that you liked it?" scratching his neck nervously, he smiled at her, who blushed at him in response.

"I loved it."

"Where is my return gift?" there came his plan. After watching all the sappy romances, he has planned this scene beforehand where the bride gets her gift and when asked for a return gift she'd have none and the groom would ask for a kiss instead and they kiss. That's what Shehryaar has planned all along, but what he didn't expect was for her to jump out of the bed and rummage through her section of the wardrobe, which his cousins have set the day before yesterday.

"What is this?" Shehryaar asked in confusion as she placed another box in his hands, he eyed her and then back at the box.

"Open it?" Leila insisted eagerly whilst standing beside him, he pulled her on his laps taking her off guard.

"What?" she gasped in surprise as he kept the box aside and cupped her face instead.

"I don't want that, I want something else," he whined making her pout.

"You didn't even open that," she complained but froze as he traced on her lips lazily and then she realized what was he up to which turned her red once again.

"I can't believe all of this, you sitting here on my lap, as my wife," he said those words whilst looking dreamily into her eyes.

She smiled whilst continuing to blush, "I know it happened too soon."

They prayed together that night, asking for a happy married life and thanking the almighty for blessing them with each other after all the trials.

That night when Leila said yes to him, he came home thinking to ask his family's permission once again. But what he didn't expect was to see all of them planning their wedding already and not even a week passed by, they are now officially nikhahfied.

"You didn't open my gift." Leila pouted again later in the night, he chuckled at her innocence," I know that it would be something which I'll love but as for now, I want this." the world seemed to freeze for the both of them as he placed his lips on hers. Finally!

He has waited twenty-seven years of his life for this beautiful moment and it was so worth it, she was numb the whole time as he nibbled on her upper lip whilst kissing her hungrily. She slowly kissed him back shyly which made him smile in between as he deepened the kiss.

And the next moment they were kissing each other hungrily, like their life depended on it.

One thing leads to the other and what followed next was the passionate union of two souls, who have longed to be together for so long and now they are one in every sense. Their journey was a difficult one but in the end, it was so worth it.

***

A month later.

Leila frowned at the bathroom door as she held the towel in her hands, she knew too well about what he is planning and she was not going to let it happen," where's my towel?" Shehryaar's husky voice was heard from inside as he held his hand out, asking for the towel.

"Here." she planned to quickly place it on and run away but he outsmarted her by pulling her in, quickly.

"You insatiable beast." she hit his chest playfully as he made her stand under the shower along with him, she gasped for breath when he kissed on her nape whilst mumbling, "what can I do? You, my wife, is so irresistible." Leila saw that coming anyway. She arched her head back, whilst shutting her eyes close giving him more access to kiss.

"No marks." she moaned as he bites on some random places.

"Too late," he whispered mischievously.

"I'm still mad at you." she pouted making her look more irresistible. The running shower has already drenched her soaking wet as the dress hugged her body, showing off all her beautiful curves.

"I'll come back, soon. Insha Allah!" Shehryaar hated the fact that he had to go on a business trip so soon after his wedding, but work was important too.

"I won't talk with you until you come back home." he laughed at her reply knowing very well how she will be the first one to call him and inquire if he has landed safely or not. That much he knows about her.

"I'm serious." Leila tried to sound intimidating but she sounded cute instead.

"We will see about that." his words were muffled as he pulled her into another breathtaking kiss. She kissed him back boldly.

He can never really get enough of her. And under his influence, she has been turning bolder day by day, it wasn't like he's complaining or something. He's enjoying every moment he get to spend with her and only he knows how difficult it is going to be for him to be away from her for the next few days.

***

Two more months later.

The days turned into months and Shehryaar still hasn't returned home, yet. Over time many things have changed in the Qureshi house. For a change Agha Jaan has apologized to everyone for his acts, he was very guilty and ashamed. They all forgave him. Armeena too has apologized to Leila, personally and admitted how jealous she was of her. Because Leila had everything which she didn't and that forced her to join hands with their grandfather to destroy the first wedding.

Leila understood her point of view and forgave her too.

And now they are one big happy family.

But nothing has stopped her from missing him. They fought a lot during this time, mainly because Leila wanted him back sooner and he was giving work more priority. It really was an important trip but she was his wife and she needed him.

She even cried the previous night when they were on a video call. She exclaimed how sad she is without him and he looked helpless from the other end.

It was just another day where everyone was doing their usual routine and Leila told everyone at the dining table to leave her alone for some time and they gave her just that.

She slept on the bed whilst hugging his pillow tightly.

"Leila..." she heard that familiar voice whisper in her ears which made her eyes open slowly," I know you're a dream. Go away," she mumbled incoherently whilst going back to sleep. He smirked mischievously at that

And the next moment her eyes opened wide in shock as she felt those familiar lips against hers. He was here for real. Lying just beside her. It felt too good to be true and if that was a dream, she never wanted to wake up from that dream.

"I missed you," Shehryaar murmured as they broke the kiss, swiftly pulling her on top of him.

"You didn't." she hit on his chest hardly but he didn't say anything to that as he was too busy hugging her tightly. It felt so freaking good to just hold onto her like that.

"I missed you more." she hugged him back emotionally and they remained silent for a while. Just listening to each other's heartbeat and intertwined their fingers together.

"Leila?"
"Hmm."
"I love you."
"Mmm."
"Leila."
"Hmm."
"I love you."
"Mmm, I know."
"Leila?"
"Yes, Shehryaar."
"I love you."
"I love you too, happy?"
"Took you long enough.

"I'm not talking with you," she whispered whilst hugging onto him more tightly, making sure if he was really here and he didn't know if he should be worried or not.

"I'm here now." he tightened the hug.

"Took you long enough."

"I'm sorry, Janaan. I can do anything to make it up to you." Shehryaar ran his hands through her soft silky hair as he said those words.

"Anything?" stressing on the word any, she asked him with a mischievous smile.

Shehryaar knew what he was signing up for when he said those words. But he will do anything for her to become his Leila again. He missed her so much and all he needed was her hug and love not this anger.
He knew too well that her anger will last only for a few minutes but still he'll do anything. Anything to make her smile at him again.

"Anything," he replied with a smile and Leila was a goner already, he has got the most gorgeous smile ever and him being her husband makes it all the more thrilling. She can ogle at him for as long as she wants. He's hers. Hers to look at. Hers to love and hers to keep.

One of the best things Leila has ever decided was this; to give their relationship a second chance. Sure there were many ups and downs in just three months of their wedding, but at the end of the day they were happy and that is what matters.

And they were glad that by Allah's grace they did get their happy ever after, but they still had a long way to go and they were so ready for everything.

THE END

Sometimes all you need is a second chance.